Original title:
Who Needs Meaning When You Have Pizza?

Copyright © 2025 Creative Arts Management OÜ
All rights reserved.

Author: Thomas Sinclair
ISBN HARDBACK: 978-1-80566-049-1
ISBN PAPERBACK: 978-1-80566-344-7

Slices of Serenity

In a box of warmth, my heart does sing,
Toppings piled high, oh what do they bring?
Each slice a hug, with flavors to roam,
In a cheesy embrace, I find my true home.

Pepperoni dreams dance on the crust,
Crispy edges call, oh it's a must!
Forget the deep talks, just pass me that pie,
In gooey delight, all worries can die.

The Crust of Contentment

Doughy delights, golden and fair,
Each bite a giggle, a joyful affair.
With every bite, the world fades away,
In cheesy utopia, I long to stay.

Sauce running wild, like laughter at night,
Pizza in hand, everything feels right.
No need for a quest, just savor the zest,
In the realm of dough, I feel truly blessed.

Saucy Revelations

Tomato storms brewing under the cheese,
Incredible flavors, a taste that can please.
Forget about quests for meaning or truth,
With a slice on my plate, I'm feeling uncouth.

Basil whispers sweet secrets to me,
Crust like a pillow, oh joy—such glee!
As grease drips down, my laughter erupts,
Let's toast to the toppings, those flavor-filled cups.

Cheesy Epiphanies

Melted wisdom flows like a stream,
In a world quite ridiculous, I'm living the dream.
With mushrooms on top, my laughter ignites,
Pizza's a treasure, it brings pure delights.

A slice of this joy, and I'm feeling divine,
Crust in my hand, I've found the right sign.
With each cheesy wink, the universe beams,
In a land full of pizza, I chase my wild dreams.

Saucer of Satisfaction

A slice of joy, oh what a feast,
Cheese so gooey, I am a beast.
Crust like a hug, warm and tight,
Each bite a giggle, pure delight.

Tomato dreams in a cheesy lane,
Garlic whispers, a savory refrain.
When life gets tough, here's the key,
Just grab a slice and set it free.

Crusty Connections

Gather 'round, friends, the table's set,
With cheese and laughter, no room for fret.
Crusty edges, our stories blend,
In this pizza realm, all hearts mend.

Saucy gossip flows like wine,
Toppings shared, oh so divine.
Anchovies? No, we stick to fun,
Under the moon, we're all as one.

Savory Stories

Doughy debates over pepperoni,
Each slice a tale, a sweet testimony.
From oven's warmth, the laughter rises,
In every bite, a world of surprises.

Barbecue dreams, veggie delight,
In cheesy threads, we share the night.
With each mouthful, bonds expand,
Savory stories, hand in hand.

Toppings on Togetherness

With every topping, we find our groove,
A dance of flavors, let's make a move.
Basil and olives, a quirky pair,
Over dough, we lose all care.

A sprinkle of laughter, a dash of hugs,
Crusty delights, no room for shrugs.
In the banquet of life, let's celebrate,
With pizzas piled high, it's never too late.

Chew on This

When life gets tough, just take a bite,
A gooey slice brings sheer delight.
Layers of joy, both cheesy and warm,
Pizza's magic can weather any storm.

From pepperoni to veggie bliss,
Each slice served with a happy hiss.
Forget your worries, let toppings reign,
In the world of pizza, there's no such pain.

Crusty Curiosities

A crust so golden, it whispers tales,
Of cheese-filled wonders and sauce-filled trails.
What's the meaning? Who really cares,
When dough's the answer to all our prayers?

Crispy edges where laughter resides,
Slicing through woes, as fun collides.
Toppings galore, with flavors that dance,
In the pizza party, we all take a chance.

Mozzarella Mystique

With mozzarella dreams that stretch and pull,
A savory siren that makes hearts full.
No philosophers here, just cheesy delight,
Life's a slice, and it's feeling just right.

Sauce so rich, it tells a story,
Bakes in the oven, then serves us glory.
A pizza pie filled with giggles galore,
In every corner, laughter we store.

Plateful of Perspectives

On a plate of flavors, we dine with glee,
A sprinkle of spice, with wild jubilee.
From thin crust dreams to deep dish delight,
Every pizza choice makes the mood bright.

As we gather round for a slice or three,
Each crunchy bite sets the laughter free.
What's life without joy, toppings like sprinkles?
Together we feast, as the clock simply crinkles.

Toppings of Joy

Saucy slices make me grin,
Cheese so melty, where to begin?
Mushrooms dance, peppers prance,
On this crust, I take my chance.

Gather round, let laughter rise,
As deep-dish tales reach for the skies.
An olive here, a laugh right there,
With every bite, we shed our care.

Doughy Dreams

In the oven, magic swirls,
Saucy symphonies, dough that twirls.
Crusty castles built with zest,
In this realm, we find our best.

Cheesy whispers tease the soul,
Twisting flavors, lose control.
A slice of joy within our reach,
Who needs wisdom? Just let's feast!

Pepperoni Perspectives

Round and red, the slices gleam,
In every bite, a tasty dream.
Funnies sprout like basil's grace,
With pepperoni, what a chase!

Crusty debates, oh what a treat,
As pineapple friends find the heat.
Life's too short for bland debates,
Just bring the pizza, clear the plates!

A Feast of Foolishness

Tomato laughter fills the air,
With garlic jokes, we've not a care.
Doughy antics make us sing,
In this feast, joy's the real thing.

Laughter served with extra cheese,
Crusty puns are sure to please.
In this moment, let's be free,
A slice of silliness, just for me!

Tasting the Unexamined

Crust so crispy, warm delight,
Cheese like clouds, pure appetite.
Toppings dance, a vibrant glow,
Each bite whispers, 'Just let go.'

Saucy dreams in every slice,
Life's a game; let's roll the dice.
Forget the world, it's just a fling,
In this circle, joy takes wing.

Whimsical Wedges

Circular wonders, doughy bliss,
A slice of laughter, can't resist.
Toppings galore, a wild spree,
In this moment, we are free.

Cheese currents melt with each grin,
The party starts when you dig in.
Pizza pals, we laugh and cheer,
Life's a feast, and love is near.

The Utter Joy of Cheese

Layers thick, a cheesy dream,
Stretchy strings that make me beam.
Savor the flavor, let it flow,
In pizza's arms, I find my glow.

Gooey riches, life's delight,
In cheesy realms, all feels right.
With each bite, my heart takes flight,
Crowned by joy, this tasty night.

Pondering over Pepperoni

Spicy circles, bold and true,
They waltz with cheese, a tasty brew.
I ponder deep while munching slow,
What is life, with pizza flow?

Each slice a riddle, savory, bright,
Fleeting moments, pure delight.
So let's not dwell on endless quest,
With pepperoni, I feel blessed.

Craving Clarity

In a world so vast and wide,
I ponder deep while I abide.
Yet toppings on my cheesy feast,
Bring clarity and joy, at least.

Why chase the stars up in the sky,
When pepperoni makes me sigh?
A slice of life is all I need,
To savor joy, not just to feed.

Doughnut Worry

With dough all round and fried so light,
I find my worries take to flight.
Glazed with joy, they twirl and dance,
In the sweetness, I find my chance.

Beneath the sprinkles, I confide,
In flavors bold, I'll take a ride.
Why dwell on woes when treats are near?
In each big bite, I taste the cheer.

Be Happy

When life's a mess, I make a pie,
A cheesy grin, oh me, oh my!
With every slice, I laugh out loud,
In oven's warmth, I feel so proud.

Toppings stacked in glorious ways,
Each bite a ticket to bright days.
Who needs a plan, or path, or goal?
When pizza's here, I'm truly whole.

Culinary Contemplation

In kitchens bright, I take a stance,
With dough in hand, I start to dance.
Parmesan clouds and basil dreams,
Life's twisted essence in my schemes.

While others chase the meaning's quest,
I'll savor cheese, for it's the best.
A sprinkle here, a drizzle there,
Who needs a map, when food's so fair?

Savoring Silence

In quietude, I bare my soul,
With crusty edges, I feel whole.
A peppered slice, my thoughts unwind,
In melted cheese, peace intertwined.

The world can shout, but I just chew,
With each bite savor, what's fresh and new.
In delectable bliss, I find my way,
Silence sings as I munch away.

Roundness of Reality

In a world of square boxes, we find delight,
Saucy dreams and cheesy bites.
Spin it 'round, the dough takes flight,
Every slice a joyous sight.

Tomato rivers, flowing free,
Oregano whispers, 'Come eat me!'
With every topping, glee agrees,
It's pizza magic, so let it be!

Pizza Paradigms

Crusty truths and toppings bold,
Are life's secrets getting too old?
Grab a slice, let laughter unfold,
In cheesy tales, we find our gold.

Slices shape our fates, it's clear,
With each bite, we shed our fear.
When pizza's near, we persevere,
A doughy hug, our hearts adhere.

Life on a Pizza Plate

Life's a plate, and here we dine,
Pepperoni dreams and a splash of wine.
With every chew, the stars align,
In crusty joys, we intertwine.

Laughter bubbles, garlic sheen,
Sauce so sweet, it's fit for a queen.
In every bite, a victory scene,
Pizza's the bridge to the unseen.

Forks in the Road

When forks appear, we make a choice,
But pizza's laugh, it drowns the noise.
With every slice, we find our voice,
In dough we trust, we all rejoice.

Choose the deep, or thin and crisp,
Every bite, a tasty wisp.
With sauce and cheese, life's one big blip,
In pizza's arms, we take a trip.

Yummy Yarns

Doughy dreams rise with glee,
Toppings dance in harmony.
Sauce like laughter sprawls so wide,
Each slice is joy that can't be denied.

Cheesy jokes piled high and proud,
With every bite, we laugh out loud.
Crunchy crust, a savory grin,
Life's little triumphs waiting within.

Pizza as Philosophy

Round like a wheel of fate,
Topped with love, it's never late.
Questions rise, like steam from cheese,
With every slice, we find our ease.

Pepperoni thoughts in a whirl,
Slicing through life's dizzy swirl.
In a world of chaos, take a bite,
Pondering life, everything feels right.

The Philosophy of Flavor

Sausage wisdom on a plate,
Garlic knots never hesitate.
Each crusty edge tells a tale,
In cheesy bliss, we shall not fail.

Beneath the cheese, a world unfolds,
Tasty truths, like dreams retold.
Basil whispers in the night,
Flavors dance in pure delight.

What's Life Without a Slice?

Crust so golden, warm and neat,
What's a day without this treat?
Tomatoes sing a juicy song,
In the company of cheese, we belong.

Banishing woes with every chew,
A life devoid seems quite askew.
In this savory realm of bliss,
Happiness waits in a cheesy kiss.

Flavors of the Unexplored

In a world of toppings, each one unique,
Strange combos await, just take a peek.
Pickles and jelly, a daring delight,
Taste buds are dancing, oh what a sight!

Doughy adventures, baked to perfection,
Each slice a story, a taste resurrection.
Forget all the rules, just follow your heart,
A quest for flavor, now that's the art!

Baked Bliss

Oven's a haven, warmth like a hug,
Golden cheese bubbling, it's all quite snug.
Crust so crunchy, it cracks with each bite,
Melting in joy, everything feels right.

Sauce like a dream, oh how it glows,
Each slice a treasure, everybody knows.
The joy of the pie, a circle of cheer,
One slice is great, but two brings a tear!

Slices that Smile

Pepperoni grins, on a doughy face,
Spreading good vibes, taking up space.
Tomatoes in chorus, singing so sweet,
Every soft bite, a flavorful treat.

Gather your friends, let's share this delight,
In this cheesy kingdom, all feels just right.
Laughs in the air, as we nibble and chat,
Pizza's the reason for moments like that!

No Regrets, Just Crust

Count the slices? Nah, we're in it for fun,
Every round crust, a victory won.
Life's too short for diet constraints,
When cheese is the answer, let's throw up our paints!

Crust so fine, we raise it in cheer,
Dip in some sauce, let's toast without fear.
With every bite, we shake off the stress,
Just pizza and laughter, no time to second guess!

Toppings on the Table

Cheese melts like laughter, so divine,
On crusty shores where our cravings align.
Pepperoni winks, in spicy delight,
With mushrooms and olives, it's love at first bite.

Each topping a tale, a twist of fate,
In this cheesy world, we savor, we plate.
Tomatoes dance wildly, a vibrant affair,
In saucy embrace, we have not a care.

Unraveling with Each Slice

Slice by slice, our worries fade away,
In cheesy dreams, we happily play.
A twist of garlic, a sprinkle of zest,
Life's deep questions put on an interesting quest.

With every pizza and crust that we munch,
Philosophy's deep thoughts get lost in the crunch.
No existential dread in this oven's embrace,
Just doughy bliss on my happy face.

Slices of Solace

In a box of joy, each pie's a delight,
Slicing through sadness, bringing pure light.
Crust so warm, it wraps me in cheer,
With every bite, I have not a fear.

A sprinkle of basil, a dash of hot sauce,
In this simple feast, I'm the boss.
Each slice a reason to laugh and to sing,
Pizza's my muse, let the good times ring!

Doughy Delusion

In a world topped right, I find my own way,
With stretchy cheese clouds, I float and I sway.
A peppery giggle, a cheesy old rhyme,
In this doughy delusion, I savor the time.

When toppings are tales and crusts are my throne,
Each bite like magic, I'm never alone.
A sprinkle of joy in each savory slice,
In this pizza paradise, everything's nice.

Beneath the Cheese

Doughy dreams lie under cheese,
Toppings dance in joyful tease,
Sauce like poetry, so divine,
Each slice a rhythm, pure and fine.

In every bite, laughter blooms,
Greasy fingers, spicy fumes,
A savory hug in every fold,
Warm tales shared, never old.

When crusty edges call my name,
I find my peace, my slice of fame,
No need for meaning, just a bite,
Pizza's glow, my heart's delight.

With every topping, a new plot twist,
Garlic knots that can't be missed,
Life's best moments, simple and real,
Beneath the cheese, I truly feel.

A Paradox of Flavor

Crust so crispy, yet so soft,
Flavors lift me, like a scoff,
Cheese that stretches, oh so grand,
In this circle, joy's at hand.

Pepperoni spirals, such a sight,
Baking magic, pure delight,
No questions asked, just cheesy bliss,
In every slice, a hidden kiss.

Anarchy in the oven's heat,
An epic clash of savory sweet,
Each bite confronts the mind with glee,
A paradox, what can it be?

Let's debate on toppings with zeal,
Pineapple or just straight-up feel,
No need for sense when taste is found,
In the chaos, we spin around.

Savory Silhouettes

Crusty shadows on the wall,
Sizzling sounds, the oven's call,
Grease drips, laughter in the air,
Pizza dreams, beyond compare.

Cheese cascades like sunlight's glow,
Toppings cover, row by row,
Life's dilemmas fade away,
As mozzarella steals the day.

Slice by slice, we dive right in,
The world's concerns are made of sin,
Beneath the surface, flavors cheer,
Savory silhouettes draw near.

Bites that giggle and wink with flair,
No need for troubles to ensnare,
In every piece, a hearty grin,
Life's best lessons come from within.

Pizza Poetics

Yeast and heat, a fragrant song,
In the oven where dreams belong,
A sprinkle here, a dash of zest,
Pizza poetry, a tasty quest.

Garlic whispers on the base,
As sauce and herbs embrace the space,
Each slice a stanza filled with cheer,
Building joy in every sphere.

Sliced emotions, crusty tales,
With every bite, happiness prevails,
There's humor hidden in the heat,
In pizza's charm, we find our beat.

So gather round, let laughter ring,
With each pie, the heart takes wing,
In cheesy lines, our pact is set,
Pizza poetics, no regret.

Caramelized Questions

When the dough is warm and bright,
Toppings dancing in delight.
Why ponder life's grand schemes?
Let's just melt our cheesy dreams.

Crusts that cradle all our cares,
Forget the world's demanding stares.
Every slice a sweet escape,
In this world, I'll shape my fate.

Extra sauce and hearty laughs,
Losing track of time in halves.
With each bite, a lightness flows,
Forget what life thinks it knows!

Oh, the flavors and textures collide,
Who needs answers? Let joy abide.
In sticky hands lies pure bliss,
Let's toast to this cheesy kiss.

Saucy Secrets

In a box of saucy dreams,
Lies the truth beneath the screams.
Dare to dip and take a chance,
The pizza's call is quite the dance!

Savory whispers in the crust,
Life's a game—play it, you must!
With every chew, we find the way,
Cheesy riddles save the day.

Garlicky hints in every bite,
Laughter bubbles, oh, what a sight!
Not a worry, just pure fun,
Under the moon, let's eat and run.

Crusty edges, stories spun,
In a world that's far from done.
Slice by slice, we chase delight,
To the pizza party of the night!

When Life Gives You Mozzarella

If fate hands you creamy cheese,
Gratefully embrace it, if you please.
Twist those thoughts, spin them 'round,
In savory worlds, joy is found.

Stretch that dough, lift your chin,
The gooey goodness feels like win.
With every topping, spice or plain,
Life's little gifts ease all the strain.

When troubles peak and stresses rise,
Melt it down, don't think twice.
For in the crunch, laughs ignite,
Turn the mundane into delight!

So when life feels like a chore,
Whip out the pizza, settle the score.
With every bite, the world feels right,
Mozzarella magic lights the night.

Flavorful Freedom

Crusty dreams and tomato tales,
Unveil the laughter, spark the sails.
Toppings here and toppings there,
Why wander far when joy's laid bare?

From pepperoni to pepper flakes,
Each slice a chance, a leap it takes.
Life's a feast, don't let it pass,
Grab a slice, raise a glass!

In cheesy whirlwinds, we unite,
Cut through troubles, take a bite.
Ovens warm, hearts are too,
With every pizza, the world feels new!

So toss that dough and stretch it wide,
In savory joy, let's take a ride.
Pizza parties, laughter flows,
Flavorful freedom—everyone knows!

Cravings of the Heart

When hunger strikes, I hear it call,
A golden slice, the perfect thrall.
Doughy dreams dance in my mind,
A cheesy love, oh so divine.

Toppings piled high, what a sight,
Pepperonis twirl in pure delight.
I toss my woes, I drop my fuss,
With each warm bite, I find my plus.

Garlic bread, oh how you tease,
My heart skips beats, I feel the ease.
A melting crust, a savory treat,
In every slice, my soul's complete.

So here's to joy on each plate spread,
No need for meaning with dough to be fed.
With belly laughs and a happy start,
You'll always find me, craving my heart.

Sauced in Delight

In marinara, I steep my fate,
Tomato magic on my plate.
With basil dreams, each swirl so grand,
I dip my crust, can life be a band?

Oh cheesy layers that stretch and plead,
A warm embrace, my heart's true need.
With every bite, I dance and whirl,
A saucy spin, my taste buds twirl.

Garlic whispers in the night,
Sizzling crust that feels so right.
Pineapple lovers, come defend,
With every slice, my cravings blend.

So here we are, with laughter to spare,
A feast of joy beyond compare.
In every crust, my dreams ignite,
I'm sauced in love, it feels so right.

An Ode to the Oven

Oh, mighty oven, you warm my soul,
With doughy dreams, you make me whole.
In your embrace, my worries bake,
A fragrant joy, I'll gladly take.

Temperature rising, I feel alive,
A bubbling cheese that seems to thrive.
Golden edges, a crispy sound,
In this warmth, my peace is found.

Pizzas spinning, a merry whirl,
Each slice a treasure, watch it twirl.
In your heat, my cravings align,
An oven's hug, oh so divine!

So let us cheer for this delight,
An ode to flavor, shining bright.
With every slice, a reason to grin,
In this cheesy dance, we all win!

Whisked Away by Cheese

Oh cheese, my muse, you melt so fine,
In every layer, pure joy aligns.
A cheddar serenade sings so sweet,
As mozzarella dreams twirl and meet.

From gouda spreads to feta crumbles,
In every bite, my heart just tumbles.
Fontina warmth, a hug from you,
In savory bliss, I've found my crew.

Pizza parties, with friends all near,
Laughter bursts and fills the cheer.
With every slice, the world seems bright,
In cheesy comfort, all feels right.

So raise a slice to cheesy love,
A gift from pizza, sent from above.
With every pull, with every tease,
I'm whisked away, lost in cheese!

The Meaning in Marinara

In the oven, dreams do rise,
A crusty base, a savory surprise.
Tomatoes dance in joyful cheer,
With a sprinkle of basil, bring the beer!

Cheese flows like a happy stream,
Each slice a savory theme.
Life's dilemmas fade away,
When pizza's here, it's a pizza day!

Toppings wild, a colorful spree,
Anchovies? No thanks, just let it be.
In every bite, a giggle erupts,
While the world outside just corrupts.

So roll out dough, don't hesitate,
A cheesy slice can captivate.
Who needs wisdom, when delight's so near?
Pizza's the vision, let's toast with cheer!

Tantalizing Truths

Rounding up the gooey bliss,
Each pizza slice is a perfect kiss.
A pepperoni art, it speaks loud,
In every bite, I'm thrilled and proud!

With crust so crunchy, it's pure delight,
A cheesy wonder makes my night.
In a world of chaos, it's sublime,
Each savory slice dissolves all grime.

Polishing off the last piece, oh dear,
Life's deep questions seem crystal clear.
Maybe it's just the garlic bread,
But wisdom's found in a butter spread!

Tantalizing truths on my plate,
Every morsel makes me celebrate.
Let's skip the lessons, throw caution wide,
With pizza love, we'll take the ride!

Cheesy Revelations

A magical mix of crust and cheese,
My heart races with every tease.
With each layer of savory delight,
I find pure joy in every bite.

The oven's warmth, a cozy hug,
While toppings twirl, and flavors shrug.
Ripe olives, mushrooms piled high,
With every slice, I start to fly!

In the chaos of daily grind,
The answer hides in every kind.
A cheesy revelation is what I seek,
When life's too hard, I just eat sleek.

So never ask for deep insights,
Just grab a slice and reach new heights.
With pizza magic upon my plate,
I'm too busy munching to contemplate!

Trivial Toppings

In the land of crust and dreams,
Where mozzarella softly gleams.
Pepperoni, sausage, even more,
Trivial toppings I do adore!

An artful pie is a slice of fun,
With flavors mingling, we've just begun.
From spinach swirls to garlic traces,
Life's little troubles leave no faces.

With each topping, a story to tell,
Like surreal dreams spun in a spell.
So let's gather 'round, friends unite,
In trivial toppings, we find delight.

So hand me a slice, let's laugh and munch,
In this cheesy world, there's joy to hunch.
Forget the meaning, just savor the taste,
With trivial toppings, life's never a waste!

A Melting Mosaic

Toppings dance upon the crust,
A canvas of delight and trust.
Cheese drips with a gooey grace,
In this slice, I find my place.

Sauce like laughter, rich and bright,
A symphony of flavors, just right.
Each bite bursts with joy and cheer,
Who needs deep thoughts when food is near?

Spinning Dough

Flour flying in the air,
Round and round, it spins with flair.
A ballet of bread under my hands,
Masterpiece crafted, no demands.

A little toss, a little twirl,
Imagination starts to whirl.
My heart is light, my spirit high,
In every crust, I just can't lie.

Spinning Thoughts

As the pepperoni circles fly,
My worries fade, they wave goodbye.
Garlic knots and cheesy bites,
Turn frowns into pure delights.

In this pizzeria, chaos reigns,
But every slice extinguishes pains.
Life's too short for solemn frowns,
Let's toss a pizza, not our crowns!

Savory Serendipity

A surprise in every single slice,
Tastes that dance, oh so nice.
Basil kisses tomato bliss,
In this moment, I find my wish.

Saucy dreams on melted cheese,
Gourmet magic, a cheesy tease.
With each bite, a giggle flows,
Forget the world, let joy propose!

The Crust of Contentment

Golden edges, warm and crisp,
In my hands, I take a lisp.
A slice of heaven, a cheesy grin,
Joy and laughter tucked within.

So here I sit, no cares in sight,
In the pizza glow, life feels right.
With every bite, my spirits soar,
Pizza love, who could ask for more?

Flavors of Freedom

In crust we trust, let toppings soar,
Pepperoni dreams, who could ask for more?
A slice of laughter, served on the side,
With each cheesy bite, we take a joyride.

Pineapple rebels, sweet and bold,
A culinary tale that never gets old.
From deep dish love to thin crust delight,
Every flavor whispers, 'You're doing it right!'

Saucy adventures, a dance on the tongue,
In the oven of life, we're forever young.
Twirling the dough, we set our hearts free,
In the land of toppings, we're wild as can be.

So raise up your slices, let friendship devour,
In this cheesy realm, we thrive and empower.
With laughter and toppings, our hearts interlace,
In flavors of freedom, we find our place.

The Aroma of Happiness

In the air, a symphony of scents,
Mozzarella magic, the joy it represents.
Basil sings softly, a fragrant delight,
With every warm waft, everything feels right.

Crusts that crackle, they shimmer and shine,
Tomato sauce rivers, a love so divine.
Garlic and herbs, a dance on the nose,
An invitation to feast, that never slows.

Friends gather 'round, with laughter and cheer,
With each tasty slice, our worries disappear.
Pizza, oh pizza, our savory muse,
In your warm embrace, there's no time to lose.

So here's to the moments, the flavors we share,
In the aroma of happiness, none can compare.
With cheese-laden joy, our spirits unite,
Together we savor, the pure pizza light.

Layered Lives

Like layers of cheese, our stories entwine,
From a sprinkle of joy to a dash of divine.
Life's like a pizza, with toppings galore,
Each slice tells a tale, a reason to explore.

Sausage and laughter, a sprinkle of spice,
Sometimes the chaos can feel oh-so-nice.
From heartache to triumph, each flavor unfolds,
Layered with laughter, our lives are retold.

The crust is the base, so solid and true,
Toppings are dreams, both the old and the new.
With friends around the table, we dig in with glee,
In this bounty of flavors, we set our hearts free.

So here's to the layers, the highs and the lows,
In this quirky adventure, anything goes.
With each slice we savor, we craft our own tale,
In the kitchen of life, we'll always prevail.

Beyond the Plate

There's magic in cheese, a sprinkle of fun,
When the night turns to laughter, our worries are done.
With every delicious, gooey embrace,
Together we gather, a jubilant space.

Beyond the plate lies a world full of cheer,
In each cheesy moment, misery can't steer.
With garlic knots twirling and friendships so tight,
We laugh till we can't, under starry moonlight.

The pizza box opens, it's a treasure chest,
In the heart of our circle, we're truly the best.
With a feast laid before us, so vibrant and bold,
In this joyful embrace, we chase off the cold.

So raise up your slice, let your spirit take flight,
In a universe of flavors, everything feels right.
Beyond the plate, there's a giggle and cheer,
For in this shared moment, happiness is near.

Craving the Unknown

In a world so vast, I chase the cheese,
With each hot slice, I find my peace.
Toppings stacked high, a glorious sight,
Forget the meaning, I'll munch all night.

Crust so flaky, it dances in glee,
Garlic and herbs, they beckon to me.
Lost in a cloud of pepperoni dreams,
Who needs a guide when the pizza screams?

Panic's replaced with a cheesy bite,
Doughy delight makes everything right.
Forget the deep thoughts, I'm on this quest,
In the pizza realm, I feel truly blessed.

Flavorful Frustrations

Torn between toppings, oh what a plight,
Anchovies or mushrooms? Which one feels right?
Sauce drips down, a spicy delight,
This flavorful war, a pizza knight!

I question my choices, but then I take two,
Each slice of schema is gooey, not new.
Life's hard enough without this stress,
So I drown in marinara, what a mess!

When toppings collide, my heart's a dance,
Like pineapple dreams in a savory trance.
In the laugh of a slice, I find my way,
So let's argue toppings, it's a fun display.

The Slice of Simplicity

Round like a circle, a beacon of joy,
In every crusty crevice, I find the ploy.
Tomato and cheese, so simply profound,
In each cheesy waft, my peace can be found.

Slice by slice, I chew on my fate,
With each crispy bite, I question my state.
In this simple joy, I feel so alive,
Forget the quizzes; it's pizza I thrive!

So hand me a plate, the world can wait,
I find my meaning, it's far from straight.
As grease drips down, I'll wear it with pride,
For in this moment, I take a tasty ride.

Sausage and Sentiments

Sausage sizzles, a meat lover's tale,
Each bite my heart sings, I cannot fail.
On a doughy canvas, emotions that blend,
In every slice taken, I found a friend.

Between layers of cheese, my worries dissolve,
In the warmth of this pie, my puzzles evolve.
With crust as my comfort, I'm ready to feast,
Let the world keep spinning, I'm tied to this yeast!

With ranch drizzled dreams and laughter as spice,
In the oven of life, I find my advice.
Each bite is a hug, a savory cheer,
Sausage and smiles, who needs more here?

The Simple Pleasures of Pie

Cheese and sauce, a tasty treat,
A wondrous dance, a doughy feat.
No need for deep, profound debates,
Just pass the box, let's clean our plates.

In every slice, a smile ignites,
With pepperoni, joy delights.
No philosophers on this divine night,
Just crusty goodness, a true bite.

An orchestra of flavors blend,
With gooey cheese, we can't pretend.
The world can spin with worry and care,
But here we sit, with pizza to share.

So grab a plate, let laughter flow,
With each warm slice, our spirits grow.
Forget the quest for meaning's song,
In cheesy bliss, where we belong.

A Slice of Euphoria

A slice escapes, a cheesy cheer,
It brings us joy, it draws us near.
No search for answers, just melted bliss,
Each savory bite, impossible to miss.

Toppings dancing, they twirl and spin,
In this grand feast, we all win.
With crusty edges, we cannot stall,
In cheesy heaven, we hear the call.

Cravings arise, it's hard to wait,
For doughy goodness on our plate.
Forget the woes, let laughter reign,
In every slice, we break our chains.

So gather 'round, let friendships soar,
In the warmth of pizza, who could ask for more?
With each shared bite, our spirits swell,
In this pizzeria, all is well.

Doughy Dialogues

Around the table, friends unite,
With every slice, we feel just right.
No heavy thoughts or wisdom sought,
Just savory bites and laughter caught.

Conversations float on cheesy dreams,
As we devour our favorite themes.
A simple meal, yet oh so grand,
In dough we trust, we take a stand.

With each topped treasure, bonds grow tight,
We share our stories, hearts ignite.
The crusty dialogue never ends,
In pizza's warmth, we're all good friends.

So let's toast our slices, let's make a cheer,
To doughy delights that draw us near.
In a world of chaos, let's simply dine,
Where pizza is life—and all is fine!

Crusty Comforts

In the oven, magic starts,
A pizza pie, it warms our hearts.
No need for rules, or logic's game,
Just cheesy joy, no one to blame.

Tomato sauce like a painter's brush,
Creating art, in a tasty rush.
A soft embrace, each crusty bite,
In pizza's glow, we find delight.

With friends and laughs, we take our place,
In pizza's realm, we find our space.
No question of why, just enjoy the ride,
In cheesy comfort, we all reside.

So raise a slice, and toast the night,
With every nibble, our hearts feel light.
No searching high, no reaching low,
In crusty bliss, we let love flow.

Melting Moods

In a world of dough and cheese,
All my worries seem to sneeze.
Toppings dance upon the crust,
With each slice, I find my trust.

Gooey layers drape like dreams,
Melted laughter bursts at the seams.
A slice shared is joy unfurled,
A cheesy bond to change the world.

A Gastronomic Guide

In the land of sauce and zest,
Finding happiness, I jest.
Pepperoni, olives, spice,
Every bite feels blissful, nice.

Crusts like cushions, warm and round,
In this feast, pure joy is found.
Forget the deep thoughts, let's chow,
Slice by slice, we'll take a bow.

Pizza Philosophers' Playground

In this circle of cheesy dreams,
Life is served with endless themes.
What matters more than a good pie?
Philosopher's hat? Just pass the slice, oh my!

Each topping tells a tale untold,
In this oven, wisdom's gold.
Forget the weight of grand debates,
With each nibble, my joy awaits.

The Palette of Possibilities

A canvas made of dough and fire,
With colors rich, they never tire.
A sprinkle here, a drizzle there,
Each creation shows we care.

Close your eyes, take a bite,
Worlds awaken, pure delight.
Why ponder life and its great quest?
Let's savor each slice; it's simply the best!

Toppings of Tranquility

Cheese piled high like a mountain,
Each slice brings joy, no need to doubt it.
Pepperoni smiles, a savory cheer,
In the chaos of life, pizza's always near.

Olives and peppers, a colorful scene,
With every bite, life feels more serene.
A dash of oregano, a sprinkle of fun,
In this cheesy world, we are all one.

Saucy Epiphanies

In the swirl of sauce, I find my muse,
Margherita magic, with nothing to lose.
Each bubble of crust, a reason to laugh,
Pizza dreams serve a slice of a path.

A squirt of ketchup? Oh, that's absurd!
Yet here I am, lost in the word.
With basil so fresh and garlic so bold,
These saucy delights never grow old.

The Comfort of Cheese

Cheddar and mozzarella, life's warm embrace,
Every cheesy joke has its rightful place.
In slices we trust, no need for a guide,
Eating my way through life's funny ride.

As ricotta whispers sweet tales of glee,
And parmesan sprinkles like confetti on me.
Crusty companions are rising like toast,
In the world of pizza, I gladly boast.

Dough Dreams

In my dreams, dough rises, fluffy and light,
Baking up laughter each glorious night.
With toppings galore, adventures unfold,
This doughy delight is worth more than gold.

Crust so warm, it's a hug on my plate,
As flavors collide, life feels just great.
Sharing a slice with friends by my side,
In the kingdom of pizza, we all take pride.

Tantalizing Taste Buds

Sauce drips down, so saucy and red,
A feast on the table, enough for the spread.
Cheese stretching wide, a gooey delight,
Slice after slice, our appetite takes flight.

Toppings galore, a rainbow on dough,
Pepperoni winks, say cheese, whoa!
From mushrooms to olives, a party on top,
Each bite we take, we just can't stop.

Crust that is crispy, a perfect embrace,
With every warm nibble, we quicken the pace.
We laugh and we munch, life's trivial cheer,
Why search for meaning when pizza's right here?

So let's raise a slice, a toast to the night,
With cheesy adventures, our hearts feel so light.
No ponderous thoughts, just laughter and fun,
In a world full of pizza, we know we have won.

Bliss Beneath the Cheese

Under the cheese, such happiness lies,
Crust in the oven, a glorious surprise.
Garlic and herbs serenade hungry hearts,
When it's time for pizza, oh how the joy starts!

Eating it hot, a true slice of bliss,
Melty and warm, it's hard to resist.
Pepper flakes dance to the rhythm of glee,
Oh, let's keep munching, just you and me!

Tangled in flavors, a loving embrace,
There's no life dilemma on this tasty base.
Life's complexity melts, just like the cheese,
When pizza rolls in, worries seem to freeze.

So, throw down your woes, let's celebrate now,
With bites full of laughter, we take a loud bow.
In this cheesy paradise, let's pierce through the night,
Encapsulated in joy, everything feels right.

The Great Pizza Paradox

A circle of joy, with pieces to share,
Slice after slice, feel the love in the air.
It's deep, it's thin, it's a flavorful scheme,
How can we ponder when pizza's a dream?

Of crusts and toppings, a mystery unfolds,
Each bite a riddle, every mouthful bold.
What's the meaning of life, we ask with a grin,
Yet pizza unravels, where fun does begin.

Ham or anchovies? It's all just a play,
The beauty of toppings in a colorful way.
Between cheese and sauce, the answer feels near,
Just grab a good slice and toast with some beer!

So, laugh at the cosmos, let logic take flight,
As cheese melts away all the worries at night.
In the realm of pizzas, we find our own path,
Laughing in slices, avoiding the math.

Melted Moments

In a world full of chaos, let's slice through the noise,
Hot cheese and toppings always bring us joys.
A bite here and there, we stumble with glee,
Moments of madness, as happy as can be.

With saucy adventures upon every crust,
Embrace the good times; in pizza we trust.
Bouncing around, like toppings in flight,
Every shared slice makes the evening feel bright.

Friends gathered 'round, laughter fills up the space,
Pizza's a treat that no one can replace.
For pleasure is simple, it's circular bliss,
In each melted moment, we find happiness.

So let's break the bread, let joy take the lead,
Among all the toppings, it's comfort we need.
Wrapped in this warmth, we find quite the throng,
Full in our hearts, right where we belong.

Saucy Soliloquies

In a world where toppings reign,
Cheese dances like a wild train.
Pepperoni sings a tune so bright,
As we share laughter late at night.

Garlic knots join in the fun,
With crusty laughs, we get it done.
Tomato sauce spills tales so grand,
Creating memories, hand in hand.

Pineapple's sweet, we don't complain,
In this cheesy joy, we entertain.
Each bite tells a story untold,
Pizza love, worth more than gold.

So grab a slice, let spirits soar,
In this circle, we crave for more.
Mirth served hot, on a bubbling dish,
Pizza paradise, our secret wish.

In Crust We Trust

Beneath the cheese, a treasure lies,
In crispy dough, our hope defies.
Load it high with all the treats,
In crust we trust, our joy repeats.

Anchovies glint with ocean's kiss,
While olives add a salty bliss.
Crowned with herbs that twirl and leap,
Beneath the stars, our dreams we keep.

Sauce erupts like laughter's gleam,
Cheese melty, like a gooey dream.
In this circle, we share our fate,
With slices shared, we celebrate.

So here's to pies, of every kind,
In laughter's warmth, our hearts entwined.
The world's a stage, and we play nice,
A cheesy twist in every slice.

Gooey Goodness

Oh, gooey goodness, dripping delight,
A cheesy wonder in each bite.
Toppings tumble like clumsy falls,
In this cuisine, fun never stalls.

A dance of flavors, sizzling hot,
This circle of joy is all we've got.
Friends gather round with eager grins,
In cheesy worlds, our laughter spins.

Sauce like laughter, spreads so wide,
Mushrooms hop, taking us for a ride.
With every crunch and every taste,
Time flies fast; there's no need to waste.

So raise a slice to this merry feast,
In every corner, we find a beast.
Gooey goodness, our heart's true song,
In this pizza world, we all belong.

Intersections of Ingredients

In a realm where flavors collide,
Tomato and basil take a joyful ride.
Mushrooms waltz with a cheese parade,
Creating chaos, never delayed.

Pepper and onion, a spicy dance,
Each ingredient takes a chance.
Together they weave a tale so bright,
In this savory universe, pure delight.

Crusty edges, golden and warm,
In this flavor storm, we transform.
Nothing matters but this savory mix,
As forks collide and laughter clicks.

So gather round this savory art,
With each slice served, we share our heart.
In this pizza realm, we find our glee,
A tasty journey, forever free.

Savory Existentialism

Cheese pulls like fate's embrace,
Dough rising in a fluffy space.
Sauce drips like tears of joy,
Toppings dance, no need to ponder.

Crust holds secrets, crisp and warm,
Each slice calms the chaotic swarm.
Questions fade with every bite,
Life's a feast, feels oh so right.

Toppings clash in vibrant spree,
For every craving, there's a key.
Saucy truths we won't unearth,
In each pizza, find rebirth.

Beneath toppings, we unite,
Philosophy with every bite.
So laugh and chew, let worries cease,
In cheesy bliss, there's only peace.

Pepperoni Philosophy

In a world of crust and cheese,
Pondering flavors, take it ease.
Circular thoughts on a flat plate,
Let's question life—hold the fate.

Pepperoni smiles, grease-filled charm,
Drowning stress on the doughy farm.
Existence served in cheesy stacks,
Dare to dive, forget the facts.

Each slice a journey, round and round,
Finding wisdom where cheese is found.
Sausage wisdom on melted gold,
Every nibble's better when bold.

So grab a slice, don't hesitate,
Let spicy thoughts alleviate.
Forget the quest for deep insight,
Life's confusing, but pizza's right.

A Bite of Bliss

Crusty edges, warm embrace,
In each bite, a happier place.
No quandaries at flavor's door,
Just endless joy we can explore.

A splash of sauce, a cheese cascade,
Finding joy with every trade.
Hot from oven, looking divine,
Life's questions fade, like tasty wine.

Basil whispers sweet delight,
Garlic bread keeps hearts alight.
Simple pleasures on a plate,
In each morsel, we celebrate.

So stack up slices, find your bliss,
Forget the questions, steal a kiss.
Every crust tells a tale we hear,
In this moment, all's perfectly clear.

The Art of Delicious Distraction

When the world weighs on your mind,
Cheese and toppings are well-designed.
Crust as a canvas, flavors blend,
A bite of joy, and troubles suspend.

Saucy debates with peppery twists,
Philosophical pizza, none can resist.
Melting thoughts in the oven's heat,
Who needs answers when cravings meet?

Each slice a question, each bite a cue,
Engage your palate, let it break through.
Doughy distractions, laughter in steam,
With every chew, find a new dream.

So laugh out loud, and pass the pie,
Forget your woes, just let 'em fly.
Life's a banquet, let's make it grand,
In cheesy distractions, together we stand.

www.ingramcontent.com/pod-product-compliance
Lightning Source LLC
Chambersburg PA
CBHW072218070526
44585CB00015B/1399